Fishing Off the Wharf

by Don Long
photographs by Karen Angus

Ready to Read
Learning Media
Wellington

Dad and I love to go fishing together.
First thing on Saturday morning
he picks me up from Mum's.

We drive around to the rocks
to get mussels for bait.

Next we make some "chum",
for catching the herrings.
We open the mussels over a bucket
to catch all the juice.

We mix in mouldy bread
and other scraps that Dad has saved.

Then we drive to the wharf.

It's great fun down at the wharf.
There's always something happening.

A lot of people go there to fish —
Maori people, Samoans, Cambodians . . . .
We say, "Kia ora!" "Talofa!" and "Hi!"
to our friends.

First, we bait our hooks with tiny bits of mussel.

Then we flick out some chum . . .
and the herrings go mad.
All you have to do is throw in your line
and you'll catch heaps.

As soon as we've got about twenty fish,
that's it.
We can't eat more than that.
We pack up and head for home.

We carry the herrings home
in a bucket of sea water
to keep them fresh.
Dad always moans when the water slops
on to the floor of the car.
I just say,
"We should get a bucket with a lid!"

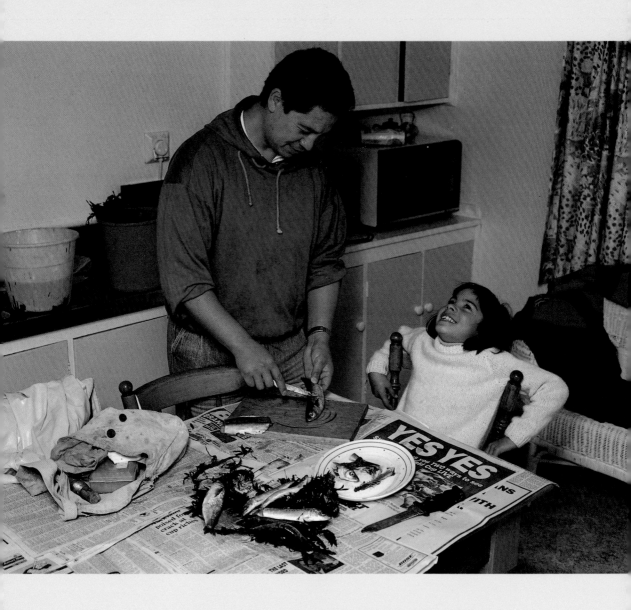

Dad scrapes off the scales,
then guts the fish.
He slices them open
and pulls out the insides.
I'm glad I don't have to do that!

The cat loves it
when we bring herrings home.

There's nothing better than fried herrings
and chips.
We cook the chips in the oven,
and fry the herrings in a big pan.

Dad gives me half,
but he always ends up finishing mine.

He says that when I get older
we should buy a boat.
But I reckon the wharves are just fine.

And I know what you're thinking!
What do we do when the herrings aren't biting?

PLIMMERTON FISH SUPPLY 'MENU'

FISH		POTATO FRITTERS	.40	FISH DINNERS		HAMBURGERS	
HOT DOGS	$1.40	SPRING ROLLS	$1.40	FILLET CRUMBED OR		BEEF BURGER	$2.50
SAUSAGES	$1.20	CURRY ROLLS	$1.40	BATTERED	$6.50	EGG BURGER	$3.00
CORN COB	$1.20	MUSSEL FRITTERS	$1.20	GRILLS		HAWIIAN BURGER	$3.00
PAUA FRITTERS	$1.20	BACON FRITTERS	$1.20			GIANT BURGER	$4.50
PINEAPPLE FRITTERS	$1.20	CORN FRITTERS	$1.20	MIXED GRILL & CHIPS	$7.00	STEAK BURGER	$4.00
CHICKEN QUARTERS	$3.00	OYSTERS DOZ	$12.~	BACON & CHIPS	$6.00	GIANT STEAK	
MEAT PATTIES	$1.20	FILLET OF FISH		EXTRAS		BURGER	$5.50
CRABSTICKS	$1.20	DONUTS	$5.00	EGG, PINEAPPLE	.50	BACON BURGER	$4.50
SQUID RINGS	.50		$1.00	ONION, TOMATO		CHEESEBURGER	$3.00
				CHEESE			

MUSSEL $5.00

CHIPS ONLY $1.50
MINIMUM ORDER FRITTERS & CHIPS $2.00

CHIPS WITH ORDER $1.20
MINIMUM ORDER WITH BURGERS $1.50

ALL PRICES INCLUDE GST

Fish and chips, of course!